Australian Bushwalk

and
Other Children's Meditations

Australian Bushwalk

and
Other Children's Meditations

Stephanie Goulter

Contents

Australian Bushwalk 1

Kangaroo Mob 5

Gum Leaves 9

Growing Tall 11

Floating Downstream 13

Sandcastles 17

Rockpools 21

Aurora Australis 25

Our Night Sky 29

Storm 31

Dawn 35

Koala 39

Platypus 41

Seaweed 45

Autumn Leaves 49

Soap Bubble 51

Australian Bushwalk

Find a safe space to be in. Close your eyes.

You're going on a bushwalk today! The sky is blue, the ground is dry and you can smell eucalyptus gum leaves all around you.

Breathe in slowly. Then breathe out.

The start of the walking track is easy, so you run ahead of the others to explore. You hear the dry pebbly path crackle under your shoes. The track ahead of you bends around to the right. You slow down because Mum says you've got to be able to see her if you look back over your shoulder.

Breathe in slowly, hold it at your heart and then breathe out.

Soon the others catch up and you race off ahead again. On one side of the track there are two huge boulders of sandstone jutting out from the cliff beside you. The sandstone boulders make a little cave, almost like a little house. You know the others are near so you climb up into the cave entrance. Don't worry, you haven't gone inside yet!

Breathe in. Now let that breath go whenever you like.

Inside the little cave you can see lots of green ferns. The air in here is cool and refreshing. You got hot with all that running around earlier. In fact, you might even be a little bit puffed.

Breathe in slowly and breathe out.

You hear the others getting really close now, someone pops their head inside the cave and says they'll wait for you to look around. The adults sit down and have a drink of tea from a thermos flask. You know you've got heaps of time to explore! Inside the cave is quite bright, now your eyes have got used to it. The green leafy ferns seem to shimmer from the pale light and the air in here looks tinged with green - it's a green room for you!

Breathe in and breathe out.

You put one of your hands up to touch the cave wall and your palm feels damp. Rubbing your hands over the wall you feel some water wash under your palms, it feels nice and refreshing. You wash your face and feel happy. Where is the water running to?

Breathe in slowly and then let it go.

You look down near your feet and it looks like a little stream is forming. It leaves the cave by running out under one of the giant sandstone boulders near the entrance. You think you'll follow it out and then have a drink and something to eat with the others.

Breathe in. Now breathe out.

Today's walk has only just begun but it's already been so fun. You never know what happy feeling you'll discover if you explore.

Breathe in slowly. Now breathe out.

Kangaroo Mob

Find a safe space to be in. Close your eyes. Relax your limbs.

Breathe in and then breathe out.

You're doing really well.

Breathe in. Hold it. Now breathe out.

It's time to relax. You've been very busy recently so let's go for a walk!

Grassy hills are good for walking up and rolling down. Are you ready?

Breathe in. When you're ready, breathe out.

It's not very hot yet, in fact it's early morning and school feels hours away still. You run down a long driveway and open a paddock gate. Remember to close it after you walk through! The long grass tickles your knees as you walk into the paddock and up a gentle slope. You hear a kookaburra laugh its morning laugh and a magpie carols in reply.

Breathe in. Breathe out.

You crouch down when you reach the top of the grassy hill, you're not even puffed yet! You wonder how quickly you can roll down the other side of the slope. Let's find out! Ready -

steady - go! The grass tickles your face as you roll downhill and your arms feel like windmills as you reach the bottom!

Breathe in. Breathe out. Phew!

You see the light blue sky above you and the sun peeps through the gum leaves high above you. You don't want to get up yet, you feel so relaxed here on the ground. You hear a movement near you and you turn your head slightly to see what made the noise. You breathe in and wait. Breathe out slowly and quietly. A kangaroo has crawled out through the gum trees near you, looking for some grass to eat. You don't want to move at all now, you don't want to scare the kangaroo. You hear more noises and one, two, three more kangaroos join the grassy picnic. You've been discovered by a kangaroo mob!

Breathe in. Breathe out.

The first kangaroo lies down under a gum tree and you watch to see what happens next. A little arm reaches up out of the kangaroo's pouch and then another arm pulls up strongly. A head pops up and a joey climbs out of its mother's pouch. You feel very gentle watching the joey climb out onto the ground.

Breathe in. When you're ready breathe out.

The joey hops forward and stretches out its strong back legs. It starts to nibble at the grass near the other kangaroos, they're its family members. Its mother looks relaxed and you know the joey's just like you, learning to do new things everyday before going home for a nap.

Breathe in. Breathe out.

You think you'd like to stay here all day to watch the joey play.

Breathe in. Breathe out.

Breathe in. Breathe out.

Gum Leaves

Find a safe space to be in. Close your eyes.
Do you feel relaxed?
Breathe in quietly. Breathe out quietly.
Breathe in slowly and hold it at your heart for a
moment. Now let that breath go.
Let your body breathe in its own time.
Do your shoulders feel soft?
Move them up to your ears - see if you can
touch your shoulders to your ears. Give your
shoulders a gentle wiggle. Do they feel softer
now?
Breathe in slowly. Now breathe out.
Imagine you're in your school playground and
you can see a new tree. It's a big, tall tree. You
can see patches of blue sky between its
leaves. It must be very high to touch the sky.
Breathe in quietly. Now let it go.
You walk closer to see if the tree really does
touch the sky. When you get closer to the tree
it covers you with its shade. You feel safe and
cool so you sit down under the tree and lean
your back against the tree's trunk.
Take a breath and relax.

The tree feels nice against your back so you lean a little closer. The tree has your back and you feel quite snug. As you breathe in you can smell the tree's leaves, up high near the sky. Its leaves smell clean and fresh and bright. You look up and see green leaves falling down towards you, like a green cloud coming down to ground.

You breathe in again and you know now the smell is from the gum leaves. It's a eucalyptus tree you sat down with! Well done you.

The gum leaves are still falling down in a quiet swirl. You look down at the ground and there is a carpet of green eucalyptus leaves all around you. They smell very strong and clean so you take another breath.

It feels good to smell the gum leaves so you take another deep, refreshing breath and hold it at your heart, before you let it go.

Send your quiet thanks to the tree.

When you take another breath you can open your eyes slowly.

Wiggle your toes. Then wiggle your fingers. Breathe in again and let it go. That feels better! Enjoy whatever you choose to do next today.

Growing Tall

Find a safe space to be in. Close your eyes.
Can you feel your body breathe a long quiet breath out as you start to relax?
Breathe in slowly. Now let that breath go.
Breathe in again quietly and let it go too.
Wiggle your toes.
Breathe in and then hold it at your heart for a moment before you let it go softly.
Well done.
Imagine you're a gum nut, curled up in the ground. The soil around you is good soil, not too wet, just right. It feels like the right time for you to start to grow now.
Imagine your feet are growing roots into the soil beneath you. Breathe in softly and let it go.
You can see leaves unwind above you. Your leaves stretch out and try to reach the blue sky nearby. As you grow up, tree leaves and branches reach out to other trees to say hello. You're having a friendly tree get-together. When a soft, gentle breeze blows through your leaves you hear the whispers of your friendly

tree neighbours. How nice it is to have others to share your feelings with.

Breathe in slowly. Breathe out softly.

Take another breath and go back down your trunk, back to the ground holding you safe. You feel your tree roots grow deeper underground.

Breathe in, hold it at your heart and breathe out.

Wriggle your fingers. Do you feel safe and secure? Wriggle your toes.

Breathe in again.

What a strong tree you have become. Well done.

Floating Downstream

Find a safe space to be in. Close your eyes.

Are you okay? Put your hands next to you if you feel okay. It's okay to be relaxed. Can you put a hand on your body where you don't feel okay? It's okay to change your mind if you thought you felt okay before.

Breathe in quietly. Now breathe out softly.

Do you have a word to describe how you don't feel okay?

Have a think about that word while we do this meditation. You've gots lots of help along the way.

Breathe in slowly. Now breathe out gently.

Imagine you're swimming in a river. You know it flows to the ocean, that's where all the surfers go!

Breathe in a happy breath. Now let it go happily.

The water feels cool and calm around you. Some trees are planted by the river, on the river bank. Maybe the trees are casuarinas, native trees a bit like pines. The water in the shade of the trees is even cooler than where you were before. It feels good to be calm and quiet beneath the trees in the water.

You choose to float on your back you're so relaxed. The river starts to move you over to the sunny side. Don't worry! You have your floaty devices around your arms if you need them, you'll be alright. You take a breath and relax again.

You look up at the sky. White clouds look like fluffy pillows in the bright blue sky. You hear a magpie chortle nearby. The river has your back. You can feel you're floating down the river and that's just fine. You float past a log, you float past a new shady tree, you float under a cloud high in the sky. It looks like a horse's tail, all wispy and long. It's called a mare's tail, that type of cloud. You see a kookaburra perched in a gum tree. Right now everything is just fine. You take a breath and let it go gently.

You feel your feet crinkle at the edge of a sandy little beach by the river. You take a breath and hold it at your heart for a moment and then you let it go. The sand is yellow. It looks so neat you want to get out and build sandcastles. The river has brought you here for a treat!

What a nice ride you've had on the river.

Breathe in as you wriggle your toes. Breathe out and then wriggle your fingers. Well done you, have fun building castles!

Sandcastles

Find a safe place to be in. Close your eyes.

Breathe in slowly and when you feel ready breathe out.

Today is a beautiful day. Let's go outside! Grab a bucket and leave your shoes behind!

Breathe in. Breathe out.

Someone locks the front door and you walk together across the sandy lawn. It feels spongy and cool beneath your feet.

Breathe in slowly. Hold that breath at your heart and then breathe out.

You both walk on the grassy bit when you reach the pavement. The concrete's hot today! There are pale purple petals on the grass under the huge jacaranda tree. When you get to the bottom of your street you walk over a sandy path between the rolling dunes.

Breathe in and then breathe out.

Do you feel happy when you see the beach? You feel the bucket start to swing in your hand and you let go of your big person's hand as you both start to run to the water's edge!

Breathe in and then breathe out when you like.

Sitting down on the hard damp sand you dig with your hands to fill up your bucket. Soon enough you're patting the top of the sand down so it's packed in nice and firm and flat. You can start to build now!

Breathe in, hold it for a moment and then breathe out.

Lift up your bucket with both hands. It's so much heavier now than it was when it was half-full! Well done you. Quickly, turn the bucket UPSIDE DOWN and push it onto the sand. You've started your sandcastle!

Take a moment to breathe and imagine what your sandcastle will look like. Breathe out.

Look out at how the waves are running in the sunlight. Now you know your sandcastle needs a moat and more towers! Filling the bucket is so rewarding. You make a second tower and then a third follows. You really like how the bucket feels solid when it's full.

Breathe in and then breathe out.

Add as many towers as you want. It's your sandcastle. Time to join the sandcastle to the sea! You realise you can use the bucket like a tractor to dig a trench down to the sea. You dig a wobbly circle around your towers as a moat. It's quite hard work!

Breathe in slowly and breathe out.

A wave comes halfway up the trench you've dug and then the next wave reaches even closer to your sandcastle. Finally the waves run all the way up to meet the moat.

Breathe in slowly and then breathe out.

When the water fills the wobbly circle you sigh with happiness. Well done you on all your hard work. You love how the wave chatters as it rushes around the towers.

Breathe in and then breathe out whenever you like.

What a good job you've done! The waves chase you up the beach. You race the water in the trench back to the castle moat and watch the wave surf over your shortest tower. You jump over the sandcastle before it collapses in the bigger waves.

What a good day it's been! Wriggle your clever toes and feel your happiness at all you have achieved. Breathe in. Breathe out. Now wriggle your clever building fingers. What a good day.

Rockpools

Find somewhere safe to be in. Close your eyes. Breathe in slowly and then let it go quietly.

Today you're at the beach! The sand is warm, but not too hot, and there are cotton wool clouds high up in the sky. Breathe in. Breathe out.

The sky is almost the same colour blue as the sea in front of you. Everything looks very big. Breathe in. Breathe out.

Someone says it's time to go for a walk and explore, so you all pop your towels over your shoulders and go for a lazy summer stroll. Breathe in. Slowly, breathe out.

The sand really does feel nice under your feet so wiggle your toes and feel them sink deeper into the cooler sand below the surface. A seagull runs in front of you and you follow its footprints in the wet sand. There are rocks in front of you.

You start to run to the rocks, you're so happy you get to climb something today like a mountaineer! When you touch the first rock it feels warm and damp and you can smell salty air. Breathe in. Now breathe out.

You reach up with one hand and start to climb up the rocky sea wall. You're curious to find what is on the other side of the damp rocky wall.

When you reach the top, you stop. There are little pools at the top of the rocky wall. Someone says it must be low tide if the pools are left up high. Breathe in. Breathe out.

You crouch down and look into the nearest pool. It's not the biggest but it's not the smallest either. You can see right to the bottom, the water is so clear. What do you see?

Seaweed is there, near the bottom and it's draped over some of the other rocks nearby. Tiny little fish dart in and out of the seaweed at the bottom of your rockpool. You feel happy looking at them play in the seaweed trees. Breathe in quietly, hold it at your heart and then breathe out.

You lean closer to the surface of the water and something scurries away on the sandy bottom of the rockpool. It's a hermit crab! It must be very shy to hide from you. Breathe in. Breathe out.

You look at the surface of the water, it is very still, there are no waves here. Everything feels very safe and sheltered. Everything here looks very small, not like the beach and the great big sky at all. Breathe in. Breathe out.

You hear the waves behind you, the sun warms your back. Everything is calm and easy. Wiggle your toes. It's time to come back from the rockpool. Breathe in again and then breathe out.

Breathe in. Now let everything go as you breathe out.

Aurora Australis

Find a safe space to be in. Close your eyes.
Breathe in. Now breathe out.
Breathe in again, hold it for a moment. Now
breathe out.
Imagine it is deep winter, cool and dark and
quiet. The night sky looks like black paint from
a paint box. Silver stars, blue stars and even
red stars twinkle down at you from high up
and far away.
Breathe in. Breathe out.
The moon is a skinny crescent, it looks like a
wonky, lopsided capital letter 'C'. Is the man
on the moon waving down at you?
Breathe in and then breathe out.
You look out, straight ahead of you, past the
back fence, past the gum trees, past the
ocean. Is there a stretch of green between the
sea and the moon?
The streak of green starts to swirl, like a
gymnast's ribbon and you watch the huge
green ribbon wind its way through the sky.
Another colour starts to shimmer softly, pink

perhaps, or orange. It falls down between the giant green ribbon and the ocean.

Breathe in calmly and breathe out slowly.

The two colours start to dance together, making different shapes like a giant's artwork in the sky. The stars twinkle brighter, like they have come closer to you to watch the paintbox colours swirl all over the deep, dark night sky.

Take a breath and hold it at your heart. Now let it go.

A third colour joins the other two and now all three colours now tumble together in giant waves. The colours don't blend together but share the space, they don't fight each other at their edges. Each colour has its own space.

As you watch the colours dance between the ocean and the sky you feel happy. The ground starts to feel cold under your feet it's so late. Isn't it great you've been allowed to stay out late to watch the dancing colours?

What a treat. You look up at the moon and the colours start to slow right down. The moon glows brighter in the bigger darkness. You know these night sky colours will be back and you'll be waiting.

Take a breath in and let it go.

You've been watching the Southern Lights that shine beneath the Southern Cross. They belong here and so do you.

Breathe in and breathe out. Wiggle your toes.

Breathe in, wiggle your hands as you breathe out.

Our Night Sky

Find a safe space to be in. Close your eyes and take a quiet breath. Let that breath go quietly.

Take another breath. Let that breath go.

Imagine you're looking up at the night sky sitting with your family next to a fire. Are you camping? Or maybe you're in your backyard?

The night sky looks very big and very black - except for the long fat strip of our Milky Way.

You hear the fire crackle near you and the heat is just right - not too hot, not too cold. It's just right for you.

A bright star twinkles up above you and your eyes twinkle back at it. Is the bright star red? Is it blue? Or is it white? Take a moment to see which star has twinkled most at you.

Slowly breathe in. How did the star's colour make you feel? Breathe out. Breathe in and hold it at your heart. Breathe out.

Gently, wriggle your toes. Slowly roll over onto one side and sit up quietly. Are your eyes open?

Don't worry if you didn't see a star today, maybe it's shooting down right towards the ground!
Have a beautiful day and night.

Storm

Find somewhere safe to be. Close your eyes. Breathe in slowly and breathe out.

Everything seems very still now, everything is quiet. This would feel fine if it were night-time, a quiet time to watch the stars. Except it's hometime! The birds are quiet, the leaves on the trees are quiet, everything except the kids leaving school is quiet.

Take a breath in, hold it at your heart and then let it go.

You walk home slowly, your legs feels heavy and your bag feels too big for today. You can't wait to take it off when you get through the front door at home.

Breathe in and then let it go.

A breeze ruffles the hair by your face. It feels active and lively, like a breeze that wants to lift you up like an Autumn leaf so that you can run and twirl.

Breathe in slowly, take it to your heart. Hold it for a moment and then let it go when you're ready.

You hear the leaves in a neighbour's tree rustle and you hear branches start to creak as they rub against each other in the wind. You're almost home now, not to worry. The wind feels faster now and you really want to be inside your home so you start to run the rest of the way down the street.

You feel so relieved to close the door behind you and you run down the hall to Mum. 'No running!' She calls out and you dive in for a hug. You look out the kitchen window and see grey clouds above the tall, dancing gum trees. Mum asks you to shut the windows and puts the kettle on before the storm comes through.

Breathe in quietly and let it go.

You feel better with the windows shut tight.A crack of thunder rumbles nearby and Mum says 'you got home in perfect time.' A flash lights up the sky outside, it's bright white and high in the sky. Fat, lazy raindrops start to fall onto the rooftop. You really are very glad that you're at home now, safe inside.

The rain starts falling fast now and it sounds like lots of big drums outside. A long rumble rolls past, talking between one cloudbank to another and when it finishes Mum starts to count' One hippopotamus, two hippopotamus...' Flash! Everything outside the house looks like a giant spotlight has turned on its search beam. Mum laughs and says the storm's two kilometres away now. 'Good', you think, 'that's further away than before.'

Breathe in. Breathe out.

Mum wants you to read to her while you're stuck inside with all that rain. So you get your school bag and pull out your home reader. You think it's a bit noisy for reading but if you do it now you'll be allowed out when the storm's passed over. And that means you can put on your gum boots to jump in puddles! So you start to read to Mum and the rain starts to relax its drumming beat. 'Oh goody,' says Mum when you've finished reading, 'we've still got electricity' and you both laugh. Sometimes the power goes off for absolutely ages.

Breathe in and let it go.

'Can I go outside now please?'

'Not until the birds start to sing again,' replies Mum. She's very strict about this rule after storms, she says it means the storm's gone away for a rest if more than one bird sings. That doesn't mean it can't come back though! Breathe in slowly and breathe out.

The rain has turned into the slowest of pitter patters and a magpie starts to chortle. You jump up and Mum says 'no, that's one brave magpie. It needs a friend to answer before you go out.' So you huff a little and then the next thing you hear are three magpies and a wattlebird carousing together. Mum gives you a nod and you run outside to put your gum boots on.

Breathe in. Breathe out.

You wonder how many puddles you'll find this afternoon. Breathe in. Three puddles? Five puddles? Breathe out.

Dawn

Find somewhere safe to be in. Close your eyes.

Breathe in. Breathe out.

You wake up. Today is all sparkly and new. You stretch out your legs and your toes too. You like feeling safe and snug in your warm bed when you wake up, everything is warm and cosy. Outside you hear a magpie chirrup as it greets the new day.

Breathe in. Breathe out.

Time to get up and go outside to say g'day to that lonely magpie.

You creep through the house on tip toe, everything is so quiet you don't want to wake anyone else up. They might not understand about the magpie feeling lonely.

Breathe in and when you're ready, breathe out. You still haven't heard another bird, it really must be early days! You step outside and stand on the lawn. It feels cool and soft under the soles of your feet. You wriggle your toes again, this always helps you feel more awake!

You look out to the horizon to see where the sun might be. It isn't up yet, it's nowhere to be seen.

Breathe in, hold it for a moment at your heart and breathe out.

Then you remember that the sun is still waking up from The Other Side of the World! You feel a lot more cheerful - you beat the sun this morning! The sun must be close now, the sky that you can see is pale pale blue, in fact, it's almost white! There is a bright streak of orange under a long cloud. The orange colour is almost like a highlighter it's so bright.

Breathe in. When you're ready, breathe out.

What's that you can see now? The top of a bright basketball coming up over the horizon's edge? It's the top of the sun! Very quickly the far away sphere gets larger and larger until you can see a giant golden sphere bob up over the horizon. The sphere hangs there for a moment, golden light spreading out low and far away and then it keeps rising upwards. The magpie starts to chortle loudly and you feel all warm inside and out. A kookaburra answers the magpie and you know the day has finally begun!

Breathe in, hold it and then breathe out.

The higher the sun climbs up from the horizon the bluer the sky grows - do you need the sun to see the blue above you?

Breathe in. Wait. Then let it go.

Enjoy your new day.

Koala

Find a safe space. Close your eyes.

You're on your way home from school. It's a quiet afternoon, even the trees feel quiet today. It's not as hot as yesterday, Autumn is most definitely now.

Breathe in. Breathe out.

You reach the part of the road where the footpath finishes, now you have to walk on the dirt and grass to reach your street. You stoop down to take off your shoes and socks - you like to feel the tickle of the grass and leaves on your bare feet before you eat afternoon tea.

Breathe in. Breathe out.

You look up at the sky poking past the leaves of the nearest gum tree and you stop still in your tracks. Do you really see what you think you see?

Something quite big and browny grey is resting in the fork of the gum tree. It looks very calm, even though it sits quite high. How did it get so high without any wings? A cockatoo squawks its way past and you almost laugh.

Take a breath in, hold it at your heart and then breathe out when you're ready.

You drop your bag onto the ground and sit down beside it. You don't remember ever seeing a koala on your way home from school before! You think 'this is very…wow" and then your brain goes a little bit quiet.

Breathe in. Now breathe out.

You sit and stare. The koala doesn't blink. You stare and sit. A fluffy ear twitches. You breathe in and wait. Breathe out. The koala rubs its head against the tree trunk, slowly moving the ear you can see from side to side. You feel better. You hope the koala's ear has stopped itching now. Sometimes it's nice to stop and sit still. Like the koala in the tree, before it itched its fluffy head. Maybe you both need to eat some afternoon tea. Be still.

Breathe in. What will you think about while you're being still? Breathe out.

Platypus

Find somewhere safe to relax. Close your eyes.

Breathe in. Breathe out.

It's late afternoon, in fact it's almost the evening. You've gone for a walk before dinner and everything feels like it's getting ready to go to bed. Even the trees feel snoozy this afternoon, maybe they've had a big day too, making oxygen for you.

Breathe in. Breathe out.

You stop walking when you get to the billabong cycle near the fire trail behind your home. You sit down near some reeds and cross your legs. You're ready to wait to see what you hope to see.

Frogs are chirruping politely across the pond from you. They sound very social this evening! Maybe they're organising a surprise for you? They're really rather loud!

Breathe in. Breathe out.

A noise like water spilling out of a glass breaks through the frog song. Quickly you move your head to look closer at the surface of the water.

Concentric circles are forming out towards the reeds you're sitting near. Mum says 'keep watching, not long now.'

You hope it happens quickly now. A small dark shape glides just under the surface of the water and it doesn't make a ripple while it's swimming. It arcs its body like a dolphin riding waves and pop! its little duck bill surfaces above the water. With a wiggle a lazy mosquito is gone! Eaten up for dinner by the small dark platypus!

Breathe in. Breathe out.

Its whole body shakes from left to right as it gobbles the unlucky insect, it shakes all the way from its quivering duck bill down to the rounded tip of its platypus tail.

The concentric circles in the water grow smaller now, the platypus has dived back down to eat the duckweed at the bottom of the pond.

Breathe in. Breathe.

Mum says 'even platypuses eat their greens' and you both laugh. You hope it has a happy evening hunting insects under the pale moonlight.

'Let's go and eat our dinner' you hear Mum say to you.

Breathe in and let it go.

If it's not raining tomorrow you'd like to see the platypus again before bedtime. Mum says 'alright.'

Breathe in. Breathe out.

Seaweed

Find a safe space. Close your eyes.

Breathe in. Now breathe out.

Today you're at the beach. It's so much fun wriggling your toes in the sand. The sand feels warm and you feel happy. The sun is shining on your back and the waves are small. You feel safe and calm.

Breathe in. Breathe out.

You go for a paddle in the gently lapping waves. The water rushes over your feet and splashes up your legs. Does it tickle?

The sand under your feel feels firm and heavy, because of the water rushing over it. You wiggle your toes as the next wavelet runs over your feet and the sand feels cool and steady.

Breath in. Breathe out.

You paddle out until your knees are wet - this is the furthest out you're allowed without an adult. You throw a wave back at your adults sitting up higher on the beach. The water bobs up and down around your knees, you're deep enough for the splashing to have stopped. Something sweeps against the calf muscle of your left leg. You almost jump in fright but can't because the sand is holding you firmly now. You take a breath and feel braver than before.

Breathe out.

Look down into the water around your knees. Do you see what it was which swept against your leg underwater? Something is waving in the water near you, it's dancing like tree branches in a big breeze. Its leaves swing to and fro, from side to side and you breathe a sigh of relief. Let go of all that stress!

You're standing at the edge of a seaweed garden!

You look closer and see three tiny fish swim between the seaweed leaves. The seaweed is a home for baby fish! Clever you to see them. Give yourself a gentle pat on the back for looking so well through the water. You want to count the fish now, they look so small and pink and silver. One, two, three,....,four, five, six.

You turn around and wave at your adults again. Someone waves back. Do you want to show them the tiny fish nursery in the seaweed garden? You'll have to go back on to the beach if you do!

Breathe in. Breathe out. It's nice to share discoveries.

Autumn Leaves

Find a safe space. Close your eyes.

Breathe in. Breathe out.

Imagine you're a leaf at the end of a twig, perched at the end of a branch joined to the great big trunk of a tree. A breeze comes along and the tree's branches and sticks and twigs all sway to and fro. Every leaf rustles and you decide to let go - the breeze lifts you up and you go with the flow. You swirl around for a while, loop-de-loops, before you fall down below. Where have you come? A river? A path? A big pile of leaves? You never know!

Breath in. Breathe out.

How does the ground feel? Or has the river got your back? Either way you're safe and sound.

Breathe in. Breathe out.

Time to let gravity help you find your way.

Breathe in. Breathe out.

Breathe in. Breathe out.

Soap Bubble

Find somewhere safe to relax. Close your eyes.

It's time to wash your hands. Yes, that's right, you do this a lot, every single day. I bet there are times when you don't even remember if you've really washed your hands, you seem to do it that often.

Breathe in. Breathe out.

Turn on the tap so the water comes out in a gentle flow. The water looks clean and bright. It isn't too cold, so the water will feel refreshing. Rub your hands together in the gentle flow.

Breathe in. Now breathe out.

Your hands look wet. It's time to add the soap! If you're using a bar of soap that's great, the water washes away any germs. If you're using liquid soap that's fine but make sure you rinse it all off later!

Breathe in. Breathe out.

Pick up the bar of soap. There are already little bubbles sitting on the soap bar. They look soft and round and slightly sparkly. You rub your hands around the soap and little bubbles start to foam up between the soap and your thumbs. The soap feels slippery now so you place it back on the soap dish gently. Rub your hands together, massage the soap and water over your fingers and nails. Rub your hands all over, even the back of them, you never know where cheeky germs camp out.

Breathe in. Breathe out.

You go to rinse off the soap bubbles when a large bubble on your hand catches your attention. It get bigger and as it gets bigger it begins to change colour, from clear to blue to pink to green...and then to lavender. Wow! The soap bubble is having a disco party and you feel happy watching the disco party ball shine on you.

Breathe in. Breathe out.

You raise your hand closer to look at the disco party ball colours and you catch your breath. You see you! You're reflected in the disco part ball and the colours dance around you.

Breathe in. Breathe out.

How do you feel?

Breathe in again. Now breathe out.

Remember to wash all the soap away before you go out to play. Enjoy your day!